Spotlight on™ Social Skills
Getting Along

by Carolyn LoGiudice & Paul F. Johnson

Skills	Ages
■ recognizing and matching moods	■ 11 and up
■ empathizing and avoiding disagreements	**Grades**
■ complimenting, apologizing, and criticizing	■ 6 and up

Evidence-Based Practice

■ Pragmatic competence, the ability to use language proficiently in social situations, greatly affects the self-esteem, pride and happiness of adolescents. If adolescents are deficient in subtle aspects of pragmatic development, they may experience peer alienation and dissatisfaction with daily life (Nippold, 1993).

■ Review of research related to empathy training indicates that this instruction enhances both critical thinking skills and creative thinking (Gallo, 1989 in Cotton, 2001).

■ Targeted language intervention with at-risk students may result in more cautionary, socially acceptable behaviors (Moore-Brown et al., 2002).

■ Intervention for adolescents with language impairments may include objectives aimed at improving deficient social communication skills (Henry et al., 1995; Bliss, 1992).

■ In selecting remediation targets within social communication among adolescents, clinicians should consider the relative importance of various communication skills in terms of enhancing peer communication. Communication skills involving social perspective taking (including nonverbal language) that focus on another person are more valued by adolescents than skills that focus on the speaker's thoughts or linguistics (Henry et al., 1995).

■ Children with limited language skills experience a poor quality of social interactions (Hadley & Rice, 1991; Fujiki et al., 1997; Craig, 1993; Cohen et al., 1998). Such children have greater deficits in social cognitive processing than children with typically developing language. They have particular deficits in identifying the feelings of each participant in a conflict, identifying and evaluating strategies to overcome obstacles, and knowing when a conflict is resolved (Cohen et al., 1998).

Spotlight on Social Skills, Adolescent Getting Along incorporates these principles and is also based on expert professional practice.

LinguiSystems

LinguiSystems, Inc.
3100 4th Avenue
East Moline, IL 61244

FAX: 800-577-4555
Phone: 800-776-4332
Email: service@linguisystems.com
Web: linguisystems.com

Printed in the U.S.A.
ISBN 978-0-7606-0777-0

About the Authors

Carolyn LoGiudice, M.S., CCC-SLP, and **Paul F. Johnson**, B.A., are editors and writers for LinguiSystems. They have collaborated to develop several publications, including *Story Comprehension To Go*, *No-Glamour Sequencing Cards* and *Spotlight on Reading & Listening Comprehension*. Carolyn and Paul share a special interest in boosting students' language, critical thinking and academic skills.

In their spare time, Carolyn and Paul enjoy their families, music, gourmet cooking, and reading. Carolyn is learning to craft greeting cards and spoil grandchildren. Paul, a proud father of three children, also enjoys bicycling, playing music and spending rare moments alone with his wife, Kenya.

Table of Contents

Introduction

Adolescents who have not acquired appropriate social skills on their own are unlikely to develop those skills without specific instruction. Activities in *Spotlight on Social Skills, Adolescent* include explicit teaching, modeling, observation, discussion, role-playing, and other guided practice to spotlight specific social skill areas from different perspectives and with varying everyday situations. These activities can be presented to individual students or small groups of students with similar skill deficits.

Before beginning any social skill training, you should evaluate each student's current performance. Determine whether the student has a performance deficit (has the skills but doesn't use them) or an acquisition deficit (lacks the skills or the discrimination of which behaviors to use in specific situations). The activities in this series are designed for students who need direct instruction and guided practice to acquire and master specific skills. Use the Pretest/Posttest, observation, teacher reports, and/or personal interview to select appropriate lessons to present. These are the books in *Spotlight on Social Skills, Adolescent*:

- Nonverbal Language
- Making Social Inferences
- Emotions
- Conversations
- Getting Along
- Interpersonal Negotiation

Getting along with others may be the ultimate goal of social skills instruction. It's a topic that encompasses many things from empathic understanding to gracious acceptance of compliments. Because the self-esteem of adolescents is tied so closely to peer acceptance, the skills needed to acquire intimacy with peers often need to be taught explicitly and practiced repetitively. This book addresses some of the most basic areas of learning to understand and get along with others as well as acquiring some of the "social graces" that can make or break even the most casual interactions. These are the objectives of this book:

- identify others' moods and take their perspectives
- understand your own and others' feelings to build empathic understanding
- recognize how using kind words contributes to getting along
- avoid disagreements by making good conversational choices
- ask appropriate questions to participate in transactional interactions
- recognize similarities in situations that contain superficial differences
- give and receive compliments
- make meaningful apologies
- give constructive criticism and understand the concept of social white lies
- understand and accept the difference between fairness and equality
- answer questions about getting along in story contexts

Here are some tips to improve your students' abilities to get along with their peers:

- Learning to get along in social situations begins with recognizing basic emotional states. When students realize that their actions can affect the emotions of others, they can begin to make good social choices. Use pictures of people in various emotional states. Begin with the basic emotions of fear, happiness, anger, sadness, etc., and ask your students to identify and label each emotion. Then ask your students, "What's something that might have happened to make this person feel this way?" When students are proficient in labeling basic emotions and speculating causes for those feelings, move to more abstract and sophisticated emotions, such as joyful, disappointed, embarrassed, confused, and disgusted.

- Empathic understanding is the key to getting along with peers. One way to build empathy in your students is through unselfish service acts. Get your students involved in a small volunteer project within the school. You might have them read a story to the kindergarten class or volunteer to help younger students with a craft activity. A clean-up project around the school might also be a possibility. After completing each activity, talk about how your students' actions might have affected others. Ask them to think about how their efforts made someone else's life a little better. Have your students talk about how doing the activity made them feel and what other things they could do in their lives that would make them feel the same way.

- Encouraging students to examine the causes of emotional states in their own lives is a powerful way to develop empathy. At the top of a sheet of paper or on the board, write, "A time I felt . . . ." Then on the left-hand side, write various emotional states (disappointed, elated, amused, frustrated, embarrassed). Have students think about events in their lives that caused them to feel those emotions. Encourage them to share specific details about each event, such as the people who were involved, what words were said, and what they remember most about the feeling.

- Guilt is a great social instructor. Although often painful, guilt prevents us from making the same mistakes over and over. Have your students talk about situations in which they felt guilty for making someone else feel bad or for a mistake they made. Remind them of the importance of feeling guilty about actions, but also use the opportunity to talk about how to make meaningful apologies, how to atone for mistakes, and how to use social errors as building blocks for strengthening relationships. Tell your students that instead of avoiding someone when you are angry or feeling guilty, they should use the opportunity to talk about how the situation could have been handled differently and how apologizing appropriately might help everyone overcome bad feelings.

We hope you and your students enjoy *Spotlight on Social Skills, Adolescent: Getting Along!*

Carolyn and Paul

5

Pretest/Posttest

Read the situations and answer the questions.

1. Daniel is a good cook and he makes a new recipe for dinner. It's supposed to be a casserole but something is wrong. It looks more like soup and it smells horrible. There's no way he can serve this to his family.

    a. Circle the words that describe how Daniel feels.

disappointed	curious	disgusted
embarrassed	proud	inspired

    b. Why does Daniel have those feelings? _____

    _____

2. Marlis just finished playing at her piano recital. She had been working on the music for months and she played perfectly. She is standing beside the piano bowing while the audience claps.

    a. What two words describe how Marlis feels? _____

    b. What could have happened that would make Marlis feel differently? _____

    _____

3. Your mom tells you and your sister to clean the bathroom. You hate this chore and you don't like working together. Check each comment that might lead to a disagreement.

    ____ a. "Let's just not talk and get this done as quickly as possible."

    ____ b. "I'm not touching the toilet. That's your job."

    ____ c. "If you don't do what I say, I'm going to tell Mom."

    ____ d. "What do you want to clean first? Just tell me where to start."

Read each situation. Check each appropriate comment.

4. Your dad asks, "What do you think of my new shirt?"

    ____ a. "I think you need your eyes checked."

    ____ b. "It looks good on you and it fits you well."

5. You're visiting a friend's house and his mom served cake for dessert. The cake has nuts in it and you don't like cake with nuts. She asks, "Would you like a big piece of cake or a small piece?"

    ____ a. "I think I'll pass on the cake. I'm really full from dinner."

    ____ b. "I'll take a very small piece. I'm not a big dessert person."

    ____ c. "I don't like cake with nuts."

Getting Along with Others

Getting along with people isn't always easy. Everyone is an individual. It's tough to know exactly what makes each person happy or upset.

The best way to know whether you should say or do something is to think about how you would feel in that situation. Follow these steps:

Photo courtesy of istockphoto.com © Justin Horrocks

Before you say something to someone, ask yourself, "How would I feel if someone said this to me?"

I would feel **bad** if someone said this to me. → **Don't say it.**

I would feel **okay** if someone said this to me. → **Say it.**

Don't say it. → Think of something else to say and start over.

Understanding how someone else would feel in a situation is called *empathy*. When we use empathy, we can make better decisions about how to act. Using empathy will help you decide what to do and say to avoid disagreements and problems with others.

Tell how you would feel in each situation.

1. You spent a lot of time getting your outfit together for a party. When you get to the party, you find out you're dressed a lot nicer than everyone else. Someone asks, "Why are you all dressed up? Who are you trying to impress?"

2. Your English teacher stops you after class and says, "I didn't want to tell you this in front of everyone, but the story you wrote about your grandfather was really touching. It almost had me in tears. You have a real talent for writing."

3. During basketball practice, the coach blows his whistle and yells at you, "Pass the ball! Run the plays I give you or you'll be watching instead of playing."

Recognizing Moods ❶

Think about how the people in each situation feel about what is happening. Then answer the questions.

1. Cody really likes Martina. She finally agreed to go out with him. He picks her up on a Saturday afternoon. They get ten miles from home and Cody's car breaks down.

   a. Circle the words that describe how Cody feels.

   disappointed   thankful   sad

   amused   angry   bored

   b. Why does Cody have those feelings?

   _____

   _____

2. Antonio's team is behind by one point. There is no time left in the game. He has to make this free throw to tie the game. If he misses it, his team loses.

   a. Circle the words that describe how Antonio feels.

   embarrassed   intense   thoughtful

   nervous   joyful   anxious

   b. Why does Antonio have those feelings?

   _____

   _____

   _____

   _____

Recognizing Moods ❷

Can you tell what each person is thinking or saying? Write the letter for each quote in the picture it matches.

a. "I'll never make it through this class. Why did I watch TV so late last night?"

b. "What are you talking about? I don't need to listen to this from you!"

c. "This is so frustrating. I can't remember how to do this problem!"

d. "I'm having my best game ever. This is awesome!"

Recognizing Moods ❸

Read each situation and answer the questions about the people's moods and how they might change.

1. Deon's soccer team just won their first playoff game. Deon scored the winning goal in the final minutes. Everyone on his team ran out to hug him at midfield. Now his team will play in the championship game later this afternoon.

   What two words describe how Deon feels?

   _____

   Why does he feel that way? _____

   _____

   _____

   What might happen to change his mood? _____

   _____

2. Today is picture day and Camille is wearing a new, white shirt. She drinks a soda on the way to school and stumbles on a rock. Brown soda spills down the front of her shirt.

   What two words describe how Camille feels? _____

   Why does she feel that way? _____

   _____

   What might happen to change her mood? _____

   _____

3. It's late Saturday afternoon and Alyssa is staring at her phone. Nobody has called all day. On Friday afternoon, her friend Kayla said she was going to invite her over for pizza, but she hasn't heard a thing from Kayla.

   What two words describe how Alyssa feels? _____

   Why does she feel that way? _____

   _____

   What might happen to change her mood? _____

   _____

Matching Moods ❶

A great way to get along with people is to match their moods when you talk to them. If someone seems cheerful, talk about nice and pleasant things. If a person is calm, don't be too excited or aggressive. If a person is angry, take their feelings seriously. Don't just try to make jokes. When someone has a problem, show concern.

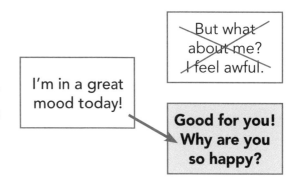

Read what each person says. Then put a + beside each comment you might make that matches the mood. Put a – by each comment that would not match the mood.

1. "What a great day this is. The sun is shining and it's Friday."

    _____ a. "Big deal. I still have to help Mom with chores all day tomorrow."

    _____ b. "You're right. It's a perfect day."

    _____ c. "Hey, I think you're starting to put me in a good mood. Thanks!"

2. "I'm really mad at my mom today. She made me wear this old coat to school and it's not even that cold."

    _____ a. "I hate it when parents boss us around. Your coat doesn't look that bad."

    _____ b. "Parents just don't get it sometimes. I'm sorry you're mad at your mom."

    _____ c. "My mom and I get along really well. She never tells me what to do."

3. "I'm worried about this science test. I don't think I studied the right chapter last night and I left my notes at school."

    _____ a. "Just try to stay calm. I bet you're going to do well. You usually do."

    _____ b. "Whatever. It's just another test. I fail tests all the time."

    _____ c. "Take a deep breath and relax. Take your time and you'll be fine."

4. "Our dog got really sick last night. He threw up about six times and now he's barely moving. I don't know what we'll do if he doesn't get better."

    _____ a. "Do you remember the time we took him to the park? That was fun."

    _____ b. "That sounds horrible. I hope you find out what's wrong with him."

    _____ c. "I bet the worst is over. It's amazing how quickly dogs get over sickness."

Matching Moods ❷

Each situation is the beginning of a conversation. Think about what might have caused each person's mood. Answer the questions.

1. "I'm so happy to see you! I can't wait to tell you what happened to me this morning. It's great news."

   What might you say? _____

   _____

   Why might this person be in such a good mood?

   _____

   _____

Photo courtesy of photos.com

2. "Listen, I don't really want to talk today while we walk home. Something happened during lunch that put me in a bad mood."

   What might you say? _____

   _____

   Why might this person be in such a bad mood? _____

   _____

3. "I'm confused. I worked on this for two hours last night and I still don't get it. I don't know what I'm going to do."

   What might you say? _____

   _____

   Why might this person be so confused? _____

   _____

4. "I am so scared. I don't want to go home tonight and face my mom. She's going to be so mad at me, I'll probably get grounded for a month."

   What might you say? _____

   _____

   Why might this person be so scared? _____

   _____

Developing Empathy: Understanding Your Feelings

Read what happened in each situation below and the things someone might have said about it. Circle the + if what the person said would make you feel better and − if it would make you feel worse.

1. You're sitting in class and you suddenly feel sick. You throw up on the floor before you can even get out of your desk.

   a. "Disgusting! What's wrong with you, you weirdo?"   +   −

   b. "Oh, you must feel terrible. Let's get you to the nurse."   +   −

2. Your cat got out of the house last night and didn't come back this morning. You don't know if you're ever going to see her again.

   a. "Cats play by their own rules. I bet she'll be back soon."   +   −

   b. "It's only a stupid cat. Just get another one."   +   −

3. You're using the computer during study hall to finish an assignment that's due next period. The computer crashes and you can't find your work.

   a. "That's hilarious! There's no way you'll get it done in time now."   +   −

   b. "Just stay calm. Let's see if we can get some help."   +   −

4. You show a picture of your parents during social studies class as part of your family tree project.

   a. "Those two really look like they're having a good time together."   +   −

   b. "Now I see why you look that way. Your mom is ugly!"   +   −

5. You are at a school dance with friends. Someone you don't know very well asks you to dance and you accept. Afterwards you walk back to your friends.

   a. "I can't believe you danced with that loser in front of everyone."   +   −

   b. "Hey, you two looked like you were having fun."   +   −

Developing Empathy: Understanding Your Feelings ❷

An important part of getting along with people is to avoid saying things that will upset them. One way to understand that is to think about how you feel about what people say to you.

Pretend you are in each situation below. Write something kind a person could say about you in each situation. Then write something unkind a person might say to you. An example is done for you.

1. You finally got the new shoes you wanted. You wear them to school for the first time.	**Kind**	*Your new shoes look great!*
	Unkind	*Those shoes look really weird on you.*
2. You're playing softball in gym class and you strike out three times.	**Kind**	
	Unkind	
3. You go to the board to do a math problem and get it wrong. The teacher makes you correct it in front of the class.	**Kind**	
	Unkind	
4. You are in a hurry to get to class. You trip in the hallway and all your books and papers go flying.	**Kind**	
	Unkind	
5. You spend extra time before school doing your hair in a different way.	**Kind**	
	Unkind	

Developing Empathy: Understanding Your Feelings ❸

Pretend you are in each situation below. Write something kind a person could say about you in each situation. Then write something unkind a person might say to you.

1. You bring cupcakes for everyone in homeroom to celebrate your birthday.	**Kind**	
	Unkind	
2. Someone walks in as you're singing your favorite song out loud and washing your hands in the school restroom.	**Kind**	
	Unkind	
3. You've been practicing the same skateboard trick for over a week.	**Kind**	
	Unkind	
4. You didn't do your chores, so you can't go to the movies with your friends.	**Kind**	
	Unkind	
5. You have a crush on someone and finally get the courage to ask the person out. You get rejected.	**Kind**	
	Unkind	
6. Your science grade on your report card dropped for the second straight quarter.	**Kind**	
	Unkind	

Developing Empathy: Understanding Others' Feelings

Use your own experiences to complete the information on the top half of this page. Interview someone else in your life to complete the information at the bottom. Compare the different experiences.

Think about when: **Explain what happened.**

someone made you laugh   _____
                                       _____

someone hurt your feelings   _____
                                       _____

someone did something   _____
kind for you   _____

someone made you feel good   _____
by complimenting you   _____

Name _____   Relationship to you _____

Think about a time when: **Explain what happened.**

someone made you laugh   _____
                                       _____

someone hurt your feelings   _____
                                       _____

someone did something   _____
kind for you   _____

someone made you feel good   _____
by complimenting you   _____

Developing Empathy: Understanding Others' Feelings

Think how the person would feel in each situation.

1. Carlos just got a new skateboard for his birthday. He has wanted a new one for over a year because the wheels were almost falling off his old one. How would Carlos feel if each thing below happened?

   a. His friends all tell him how cool they think his new skateboard looks. _____

   b. Carlos practices a trick every day for a week. When he tries to show his friends, he can't do it. _____

   c. Someone steals his skateboard from the skate park while he is in the restroom. _____

2. Alexis is on the softball team. This is her third year as a starter on the team. Her coach relies on her to play well and lead her teammates. How would Alexis feel if each thing below happened during a game?

   a. Her team comes from behind to score three runs in the last inning to win the game. _____

   b. Alexis runs as hard as she can all the way around the bases to score a run. _____

   c. One of her teammates drops an easy fly ball that ends the game. _____

3. Your mom has been working late this month. She's trying to save up enough money to buy a different car. She comes home exhausted every night, and she relies on you and the rest of the people at home to take care of the chores. Tell something you might do that would make her feel each of these emotions.

   pleased _____

   disappointed _____

   surprised _____

Avoiding Disagreements ❶

The best way to avoid disagreement and get along with people is to use kind words. Saying things that are unkind or insulting can easily cause a disagreement.

Sometimes it's hard to know whether what you are saying is kind or unkind. Here is a good rule to follow: If you wouldn't want someone to say it to you, don't say it to someone else.

Put a check in the column that best describes each comment. Be prepared to explain your choices.

	Kind	Unkind
1. "Hey, it's really great to see you!"		
2. "Go away. Nobody asked you to sit here."		
3. "What are you looking at? Stop staring at us."		
4. "You did a great job answering that tough question in class."		
5. "I'm glad you were on my team during gym."		
6. "Why do you wear that shirt so often?"		
7. "Nobody thinks you're funny. Just be quiet."		
8. "Thanks for letting me borrow your pencil."		
9. "That was a cool poem you wrote for English."		
10. "Why are you eating that cookie? Don't you think you're fat enough already?"		
11. "I'm sorry to hear about your mom. I hope she feels better soon."		
12. "I wouldn't invite you to my party if you were the last person on Earth."		
13. "Your breath smells bad."		
14. "Thanks for helping me with my math. You're so much better at it than I am."		
15. "Forget about the grade you got. I think you did a nice job on your report."		

Avoiding Disagreements ❷

Even best friends don't always agree. It's important that we talk about the things we don't agree on without arguing. Don't say things that would hurt you or make you mad if someone said them to you. Instead, ask questions, make general comments and be kind. For each item below, complete the information for you and the other person. Then follow the directions.

1. Your favorite football team _____

   Your friend's favorite football team _____

   Your teams are playing each other this weekend. Check each comment you could make that would not lead to an argument or disagreement.

   ____ a. "Your team is awful. That game will be over by the end of the first half."

   ____ b. "I hope it's a good game. It should be fun to watch."

   ____ c. "I can't wait to see you on Monday after your team gets blown out."

   ____ d. "Do you think there will be a lot of points scored?"

2. Your favorite TV show _____

   Your parents' favorite TV show _____

   Both shows are on at the same time, and your parents want to watch their show on the good TV. Check each comment you could make that would not lead to an argument or disagreement.

   ____ a. "How long have you guys liked this show?"

   ____ b. "I think I'll just go to my room and read for a while."

   ____ c. "Your show is so boring. I don't know how you can watch it."

   ____ d. "This is so unfair. You guys are always hogging the good TV."

3. Your favorite band _____

   Your brother's/sister's favorite band _____

   You two have to work together on a chore and you agree to listen to music. You each want to listen to a CD by your own favorite band. Check each comment you could make that would not lead to an argument or disagreement.

   ____ a. "That band stinks. Let's just listen to my CD."

   ____ b. "Do you want to take turns listening to the CDs?"

   ____ c. "I don't care what we listen to. Let's just get this done."

   ____ d. "Why don't you just do the job by yourself? Then you can listen to whatever you want."

Avoiding Disagreements ❸

No matter how nice you are or how well you get along with people, arguments will happen. It's important to stop an argument before it becomes nasty and personal. Here are some ways to end an argument with someone:

Photo courtesy of istockphoto.com © Jason Stitt

Agree to Disagree	Say, "We're not going to change each other's opinion on this. Let's just agree to disagree."
Change the Subject	Say, "I don't want to argue with you about this. Let's talk about something else."
Ask Questions	Instead of arguing your point, ask questions to learn about the other person's feelings, such as "Why do you like that team so much? Are they that good?"
Make a Joke	Even the simplest arguments can get nasty quickly. Lighten the mood by making a joke and changing the subject.

Role-play these situations or suggest ways to end each argument quickly.

- -

Your friend beat you badly in a game of Monopoly. He keeps teasing you about how easily he won. Now he's saying personal things, such as "Even my little sister plays better than you."

- -

You're showing some friends the new digital camera you got for your birthday. Someone says, "You're so spoiled. You get everything you want." You're offended because you worked hard to make money to pay for half of the camera. You start to argue with your friend.

- -

You're having a friend listen to a new song on your MP3 player. Someone comes over and says, "Are you guys listening to another one of those slow, whiny songs? You should listen to some real music." The three of you start arguing about what kind of music is best.

- -

You're shopping with some friends and see a great pair of shoes. You really want to try them on, but your friends say the shoes are too weird. You think the shoes are perfect. You all start arguing.

- -

You and a friend are watching a football game between your two favorite teams. Your team is starting to fall behind and is not playing very well. Your friend starts talking about how your team is a bunch of losers. You're getting offended and start arguing.

- -

Asking Questions ❶

Getting along with people means learning about them and taking an interest in what they say. Read this conversation:

Jane: My family is going on a camping trip this summer.
Mikela: I hate camping. I would rather stay inside.
Jane: We'll probably even get to go on a boat ride.
Mikela: I can't ride in boats. It makes me sick.

Mikela begins both of her comments with "I." She's not taking an interest in what the other person is saying. Asking questions is a good way to show you're interested in what people have to say.

Write a question you could ask each person below to show your interest.

1. "We just put in a huge aquarium at home. My dad is crazy about fish. He even put a baby shark in there."

   Question: _____

2. "We spent the whole weekend at my cousin's place playing this new football video game. My cousin is an amazing player. I think I only beat him once."

   Question: _____

3. "Hey, check it out. I got an *A* on my poetry assignment. I thought I would do terribly on it. I'm just not that creative."

   Question: _____

4. "I can't find my wallet anywhere. I had my lunch card in there and the money my mom gave me for school pictures. I don't know what I'll do if I don't find it."

   Question: _____

5. "Here comes Megan. She showed up late to third period today and then she spent the whole time talking to Maggie. Ms. Jenkins almost threw her out of class."

   Question: _____

Asking Questions ❷

Most people like to share information during a conversation. Asking questions is a good way to keep a conversation going and to show that you are interested in what's being said. Use questions to fill in the gaps in these conversations.

1. **Gina:** My grandparents are celebrating their wedding anniversary this weekend.

   You: _____

   _____

   Gina: They have been married for 50 years!

   You: _____

   _____

   Gina: The party is at their house and my mom is making lasagna.

   You: _____

   _____

   Gina: Almost everyone in our family will be there. We're expecting over 100 people to show up.

2. **Principal:** I want to talk to you about something that's been going on at lunchtime.

   You: _____

   _____

   Principal: You and your friends have left a big mess at your table in the cafeteria every day.

   You: _____

   _____

   Principal: Yes, you are the only group I know about that has been leaving a mess behind.

   You: _____

   _____

   Principal: I'd like you to do a better job of picking up after yourselves.

Asking Questions ❸

Good questions help you get information about other people. People like to share information about themselves. Avoid arguing questions. An arguing question is one in which you try to push your opinion on someone rather than trying to get information from them.

> **Good Questions = Getting Information**
>
> **Arguing Questions = Pushing Your Opinion**

Good question: "What subject is easiest for you?"

Arguing question: "I think math is super easy, don't you?"

Rewrite each arguing question into a question to get information.
(Hint: Begin your questions with *What*, *Why* or *How*.)

1. Don't you think chocolate cake is way better than white cake?

   _____

   _____

2. I think MTV2 is the best channel on TV, don't you?

   _____

   _____

3. Don't you think I did a great job reading that poem in class?

   _____

   _____

4. They should let people into the game who don't wear school colors, shouldn't they?

   _____

   _____

5. Don't you think the kids in our science class who get bad grades just don't try hard enough?

   _____

   _____

Recognizing Similarities ❶

Follow the directions to see how similar people are, even when they have different interests.

1. Mark likes the New York Yankees. Diego likes the New York Mets. Corinne likes the St. Louis Cardinals. Check each statement that is true about these people.

   ____ a. They all like the same team.

   ____ b. They all like sports.

   ____ c. They all like teams from the same city.

   ____ d. They all like baseball.

   e. What's something they might disagree about? _____

   _____

   f. What's something they could talk about together? _____

   _____

2. Celia likes to bake cookies with her mom. Twyla likes to make salads with her grandma. Ty likes helping his dad make hamburgers on the grill. Check each statement that is true about these people.

   ____ a. They all like to cook desserts.

   ____ b. They all like to cook with other people.

   ____ c. They all like to cook.

   ____ d. They all like to cook indoors.

   e. What's something they might disagree about? _____

   _____

   f. What's something they could talk about together? _____

   _____

Recognizing Similarities ❷

Follow the directions to see how similar people are, even when they have different interests.

1. Carly likes to go to the theater on Saturdays with her friends. Dana would rather watch DVDs with her family. Manny prefers to download films to his computer and watch them alone. Check each statement that is true.

   ____ a. Each person likes to watch movies in a different way.

   ____ b. They all think the best way to watch movies is with other people.

   ____ c. They all like to watch movies.

   ____ d. They all prefer watching movies at home.

   e. What's something they might disagree about? _____

   _____

   f. What's something they could talk about together? _____

   _____

2. Mitchell thinks heavy exercise is the best way to stay in shape. Marnie thinks walking and using weights are the best way to stay fit. Karon thinks that a diet full of vegetables is all you need to keep healthy. Check each statement that is true.

   ____ a. These people are all interested in staying healthy.

   ____ b. They all believe exercise is important.

   ____ c. They all believe in eating lots of vegetables.

   ____ d. They have different ideas about how to stay healthy.

   e. What's something they might disagree about? _____

   _____

   f. What's something they could talk about together? _____

   _____

Compliments ❶

Giving a good compliment can make someone feel great. It also lets that person know that you appreciate his or her actions. The best compliment has three simple parts.

"Mom, I really appreciate the time you take to make my lunch every morning."

Opening	Feeling	Specific Action
Mom, I	really appreciate	the time you take to make my lunch every morning.

Read about each person and complete the sentences to create two compliments.

1. Nicole dresses neatly for school every day. She smiles and says hello to people in the halls. When someone needs help, she is there for the person. She never says something bad about someone behind the person's back.

   Nicole, I like the way you _____

   _____.

   I also think it's great that you _____

   _____.

2. Chase is a great athlete. He's probably the best basketball player you've ever seen. He's fast, he can jump higher than anyone, and he can shoot from anywhere. He doesn't have a huge ego about his talent. He's just a regular guy and will play with anyone.

   Chase, I think you are _____

   _____.

   What I like about you is that you _____

   _____.

2. Your Aunt Cassie is amazing. Whenever you have problems at home, she's ready to listen and give you advice. She doesn't always tell you what you want to hear, though. If you've done something wrong, she lets you know about it. Then she gives you good ideas for ways you can be better.

   Aunt Cassie, I appreciate _____

   _____.

   Another thing I like about you is _____

   _____.

Compliments ❷

Compliments are best when they are specific. People like to hear exactly what it is about them or what they did that you liked. A general compliment doesn't mean as much.

Rewrite each general compliment below so it addresses something specific about a person or a person's actions.

1. I like your clothes.

    _____

    _____

    _____

2. You are a good student.

    _____

    _____

    _____

3. You have a lot of musical talent.

    _____

    _____

    _____

4. You are good at sports.

    _____

    _____

    _____

5. You are funny.

    _____

    _____

    _____

6. You are polite.

    _____

    _____

    _____

Compliments ❸

When someone gives you a compliment, thank the person and show that you appreciate the kind words. There are two things you should not do when someone gives you a compliment:

> **Compliment:** "Your hair looks really nice today."
>
> 1. **Don't "brush off" the compliment.** "Really? I think it looks the same as every day."
> 2. **Don't try to "inflate" the compliment.** "You're right. It does look good. It should because I spent a lot of time working on it."

Each situation contains a compliment. Put a + by each appropriate comment and a – by each inappropriate comment. Be ready to explain your choices.

1. You wear your favorite NFL team sweatshirt to school. One of your friends says, "Cool sweatshirt. That looks great on you." What do you say?

   _____ a. "Oh, I've had this thing forever. I'm tired of it."

   _____ b. "Thanks for noticing. It's one of my favorites!"

   _____ c. "It is pretty cool. I don't think anyone else has one like it."

2. You did a PowerPoint presentation for your social studies project. Afterwards someone in your class says, "Your PowerPoint was great. You really found some awesome pictures to use." What do you say?

   _____ a. "It would have been better but the teacher made me take out some stuff."

   _____ b. "I'm glad it's over. It was really boring to work on."

   _____ c. "I put a lot of work into it. I'm glad you liked it."

3. Another student's computer is frozen during study hall, and the teacher is out of the room. You're able to figure out what's wrong and fix it. The student says, "You really know what you're doing. Thanks for helping me." What do you say?

   _____ a. "I know everything there is to know about computers."

   _____ b. "You're welcome. I'm just glad I was able to fix it for you."

   _____ c. "That was easy. I'm surprised you didn't figure it out yourself."

4. After chorus class, a kid who sits next to you tells you, "You've really been singing that last song well. I'm having all kinds of trouble with it, but you sound great."

   _____ a. "Thanks for saying that. I've been practicing a lot at home."

   _____ b. "I don't know what's so hard about it. It's just a song."

   _____ c. "You should get your ears checked. I think I sound awful."

Apologizing ❶

We all do things that cause damage or hurt others' feelings. When that happens, we need to apologize for our actions. Here are some tips for making an apology:

- Apologize in person. Don't use an e-mail, a note or even a phone call.

- Apologize quickly. As soon as you know you've done something wrong, take action.

- Take responsibility. Don't just say, "I'm sorry." Tell why you regret what you did. Show that you are sorry for making the person feel bad.

- Fix the problem. If you've damaged or lost something, fix it or pay for a new one.

Put a + by each appropriate apology and a – by each inappropriate apology.

1. You borrow your friend's MP3 player over the weekend. You drop it while you're riding your bike and it breaks. What do you say?

   ____ a. "Sorry I broke your MP3 player. You know how clumsy I am. You probably shouldn't have let me borrow it."

   ____ b. "I'm really sorry I broke your MP3 player. I should have taken better care of it. Tell me how much it was and I'll pay for a new one."

2. Jessie wears her new, bright orange coat to school. She seems proud of it and asks her friends what they think of it. You say to one of your friends, "Did you see Jessie's new coat? She looks like a giant pumpkin!" You turn around to see Jessie standing right behind you. What do you say?

   ____ a. "I have such a big mouth, Jessie. I'm so sorry I said that about your coat. I think I'll just keep my opinions to myself in the future."

   ____ b. "Oh, I didn't see you there, Jessie. Sorry, I didn't mean for you to hear what I said."

3. Your sister made a special cake for a family celebration. She worked on it all afternoon, but it looks really lopsided. As your mom lights the candles, you say, "I hope that cake tastes better than it looks!" Your sister starts crying and runs out of the room. What do you say to your sister?

   ____ a. "I'm sorry if you can't handle the truth. Everyone can see that the cake is crooked. I was just saying what everyone was thinking."

   ____ b. "I'm so sorry about what I said. I know how hard you worked on the cake. I was just trying to be funny, but it sounded mean instead."

Apologizing ❷

The best way to get better at apologizing is to practice. Role-play making an apology for each situation with a partner.

You're hurrying down the hall to your next class. You bump into one of your classmates and knock all of her books and papers out of her hand.

A teacher brings in cookies to celebrate the end of the semester. As the cookies are passed, you say, "Yuck, do those have nuts in them? They look gross." You look up and see that you've hurt your teacher's feelings.

You and a friend are playing Frisbee. Your friend dares you to see how hard you can throw it at him. You throw it really hard, but it goes over your friend's head and crashes into your neighbor's front door. It cracks a window in the door.

Your mom comes into the kitchen and asks you if you like her new skirt. You say, "How come you get a new skirt? You wouldn't buy me new shoes last week."

Your dad asked you to drop some bills in the mailbox on your way to school. You forget to do it and find the bills in your backpack two weeks later. Your dad is going to have to pay some late charges.

At lunch, you and your friends are laughing and messing around. You knock over your milk container and it spills into someone's lap.

You return to your seat in class after going to the restroom. You can't find your pen anywhere on your desk. You accuse the person sitting next to you of stealing your pen while you were gone. You say, "I've seen you take stuff before. I know you did it." Then you realize your pen has been in your back pocket the whole time.

You grab your sister's denim jacket by accident as you leave for school in the morning. When you get home, she says, "Where's my jacket?" You remember that you left it in the locker room after gym class.

You invited several people over to watch a movie on a Friday night. After everyone leaves, you remember that you forgot to invite someone whose feelings will be hurt when you get to school on Monday.

Constructive Criticism ❶

Giving an opinion can be tricky, especially if you have a criticism or suggestion. You don't want to hurt the person's feelings if you have something negative to say, but you do want to tell the truth. Giving **constructive criticism** is a good way to express your opinion. Here are some ways to give constructive criticism:

- Give a gentle suggestion for how something could be done better.
- Ask the person a question to find out his or her opinion.
- Mix a compliment with a suggestion.

Read each situation. Put a + by each comment that is constructive criticism. Put a − by each comment that is just a negative comment.

1. You ask your mom, "Is what I'm wearing okay for going to Grandma's?" What does your mom say?

   _____ a. "Maybe you should dress up a little more since it's her birthday."

   _____ b. "That looks awful. What were you thinking?"

   _____ c. "Do you think those pants are nice enough for a party?"

2. You ask your teacher, "What did you think of my paper on the pyramids?" What does your teacher say?

   _____ a. "It was a very poor effort. I expected better work from you."

   _____ b. "Do you think you covered all the information I asked for?"

   _____ c. "It was very neatly done, but I think you missed a few facts."

3. Your sister asks, "What do you think of my new jacket?" What do you say?

   _____ a. "That's a great color on you. I think it might be a little too big, though."

   _____ b. "It's way too baggy. It looks terrible on you."

   _____ c. "What do you think of the fit? Is it comfortable?"

4. Your dad says, "Taste this barbecue sauce. What do you think?" What do you say?

   _____ a. "Yuck. That's really bland. I don't want any of that on my ribs."

   _____ b. "Do you think it has enough salt?"

   _____ c. "That's a good start. I might add a little more salt to it."

5. Your friend asks, "What did you think of my speech today?" What do you say?

   _____ a. "Did you feel like you kept everyone's attention?"

   _____ b. "It was terrible. All of your notes were out of order."

   _____ c. "The beginning was great. If your notes hadn't been out of order, it would have been perfect."

Constructive Criticism ❷

The "hamburger rule" is a good one for giving constructive criticism. Begin with a compliment (top bun), follow with a criticism (meat), and end with another compliment (bottom bun). Here's an example of the hamburger rule in action:

Your partner needs to make a poster that mentions three dangers of smoking for a health class project. She shows you the poster and asks for your opinion. The poster is colorful and well drawn, but it only points out one danger of smoking — lung cancer.

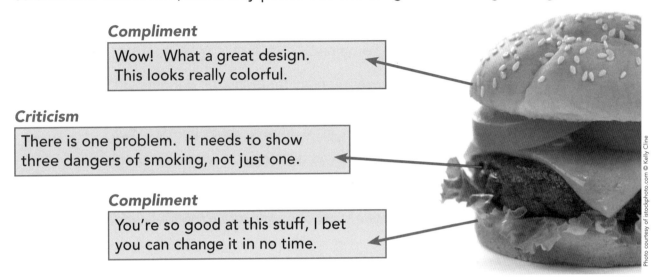

Compliment
Wow! What a great design. This looks really colorful.

Criticism
There is one problem. It needs to show three dangers of smoking, not just one.

Compliment
You're so good at this stuff, I bet you can change it in no time.

Practice using the "hamburger rule" by role-playing these situations.

1. Your friend is a guitar player. He plays and sings a song for you that he wrote. It's the first of his own songs he's ever played for you. You think his guitar playing is great, but you can't understand the words because he doesn't sing them very clearly. When he's finished, he asks, "What do you think? Tell me the truth; I can take it." What do you say?

2. You are at a friend's house for dinner for the first time. They are having spaghetti and it is a lot spicier than what you are used to eating. Your friend asks, "What do you think of Dad's famous spaghetti sauce?" What do you say?

3. Your brother is wild about a new band. He's been bugging you for a week to listen to the band's latest CD. You finally listen to it but you can't stand it. He asks, "Wasn't that CD awesome? Did you like it?" What do you say?

4. Your friend just got new glasses. They're a lot different from the glasses he had before. The other ones were plain metal frames. These are bright red plastic and are really tiny. They make your friend look totally different, and you don't know if you can get used to this new look. He asks, "What do you think of the new glasses? Pretty wild, aren't they?" What do you say?

Fairness ❶

"Fair" doesn't always mean that everyone is treated the same. Fair means that people are treated the way they need to be treated. Decide if each situation is fair or unfair by checking the correct column. If you decide something is unfair, think of a change that would make the situation more fair.

	Fair	Unfair
1. A girl in your math class has poor eyesight. She always gets to sit in the middle front seat so she can see the board. Nobody else ever gets to sit in that spot.		
2. The principal has decided that girls will go through the lunch line first every day. He says it's more polite if the boys wait until the girls get their food first.		
3. A couple kids in your English class have a lot of trouble writing by hand. The school has purchased laptop computers for those students to use during class. Everyone else has to write on paper.		
4. Too much contact with soap water makes your sister's skin get itchy and break out. Your mom says she doesn't have to help with dishes anymore. Now you have to do the dishes by yourself.		
5. Your brother missed curfew last night for the second time in a week. Your dad grounded both of you for a week because he doesn't think he can trust any of his kids.		
6. At the restaurant where you work, someone found a long, black hair in the soup. There are a few employees with long hair, but your boss says that now everyone in the kitchen needs to wear hairnets all the time.		
7. The parking lot at your school is small. There are more cars than there are spaces. The principal announces that only seniors may park on campus for the rest of the year.		
8. Your school is trying to get students to eat healthier foods. As part of the plan, vending machines will no longer sell soda or junk food.		

Fairness ❷

People get along best when they all feel like they are being treated fairly. Use a piece of paper to cover up the Step 2 portion of each problem below. Read the Step 1 information by yourself or with a partner and brainstorm a fair solution. Then read the Step 2 information. Talk about how you might or might not change your solution.

1: Late Assignment

Step 1: Lots of people in your English class have been turning in late papers this month. Your teacher has said if people don't start turning in papers on time there will be penalties. What would be a fair way to penalize people for turning in late papers?

Step 2: Does your solution treat everyone the same? Would your penalties change if you knew that the same few people were the only ones turning in late papers? Some people in class have never turned in a late paper. What happens if one of those people turns in just one late paper during the year? Does that student get the same penalty?

2: An Inconvenient Problem

Step 1: A lot of kids stop at the convenience store across from school on the way home. The owner there has noticed a lot of shoplifting lately and thinks it will stop if he limits the number of students who can be in the store at one time. What is a fair way for the store owner to limit how many kids can be in the store?

Step 2: There are often 20-30 kids around the store when school gets out. If the owner limits the number of kids inside the store, where will the rest of the kids go? Won't they cause other problems if they're just hanging around outside? Is there a better solution to this problem?

3: An Online Obstacle

Step 1: You and your brother fight about using the computer at night. You both like to get online and chat with your friends in the evenings. Your mom is tired of the fighting. She wants to have a plan to stop it. What's a fair way to solve the problem?

Step 2: Your mom is also concerned that your family doesn't spend enough time talking together. She's worried that the only way you and your brother communicate with people is through instant messaging. You and your brother don't get much time to talk with your friends during the day, so talking online is a good way to stay in touch. How could your mom's solution address her concerns about the family and still be fair to everyone?

Social White Lies

Telling the truth isn't always the best idea. The truth can often hurt someone. That's when you might tell a *social white lie*. A social white lie is a kind way to protect someone's feelings if the truth could be hurtful. Here's an example:

A friend says, "I love playing basketball because I'm so good at it."
Your friend is really bad at basketball and everyone knows it.

Truth: "I'm sorry, but you don't play basketball very well. I thought you should know."

Social White Lie: "Basketball is great exercise. I'm glad you like playing."

Check two social white lies for each situation.

1. Your best friend comes to school wearing way too much makeup. She proudly says, "I've decided to change my look. What do you think?" You think she looks terrible and fake. What do you say?

   _____ a. "That's way too much makeup. What were you thinking?"

   _____ b. "Good for you. Sometimes you just need to make a change in your life."

   _____ c. "That's an interesting look. You really made a change."

2. A friend comes to your birthday party. She gives you a strange shirt as a gift. You know you'll never wear it. What do you say?

   _____ a. "Thanks so much for thinking of me. I bet you picked that out yourself."

   _____ b. "Thank you, but do you still have the receipt? I want to take this back."

   _____ c. "I've never had a shirt like this. Thanks!"

3. Everyone has to write a story for English and read it in front of the class. Your friend's story doesn't make any sense but he's very proud of it. He asks you what you think of it. What do you say?

   _____ a. "You read your story with a lot of feeling. It was really entertaining."

   _____ b. "I can tell that you like writing stories. You use a lot of imagination."

   _____ c. "I just didn't get it. I couldn't follow what was happening."

4. You're staying overnight at a friend's house. She made brownies and you think they taste terrible. They're really salty. Your friend asks if you want another one. What do you say?

   _____ a. "No, thank you, I'm really full. I think I'll just stop with one."

   _____ b. "No thanks, the first one tasted kind of weird. Did you follow the recipe?"

   _____ c. "I don't like to eat too much before bedtime. One was enough, thanks."

Social White Lies ❷

Some people don't think social white lies are ever appropriate. They think you should always tell the complete truth, even if it might be hurtful. You'll have to decide for yourself when a social white lie is appropriate. Answer the questions after each situation.

1. A friend wants to ask a very popular girl to the winter formal. He has never talked to her before, but he's sure she'll want to go to the dance with him. You know he doesn't have a chance. Your friend says, "She'll definitely want to go to the dance with me, right?"

   What could you say that would be the straight truth? _____

   _____

   What is a social white lie you might tell him? _____

   _____

2. Your friend took you to see a movie. On the way out your friend says, "Wasn't that hilarious? I laughed all the way through." You thought the movie was lame and immature. You were bored through most of it.

   What could you say that would be the straight truth? _____

   _____

   What is a social white lie you might tell your friend? _____

   _____

3. You ask your friend if he finished his assignment for math because you thought it was really hard. He says, "I didn't totally finish it but it's not a problem. Mr. Lee loves me. I'm sure he'll give me another day to finish it." Your friend goofs off a lot in class and you know Mr. Lee doesn't like his attitude at all.

   What could you say that would be the straight truth? _____

   _____

   What is a social white lie you might tell him? _____

   _____

4. Your friend says, "Don't you think my face is clearing up? I've been using a really expensive acne medication for the last couple of days." You don't notice any change in your friend's face. Your friend still has a lot of pimples.

   What could you say that would be the straight truth? _____

   _____

   What is a social white lie you might tell the person? _____

   _____

Getting-Along Stories ❶

Read the story and answer the questions.

"Did you see the skirt Tia was wearing today?" Ashley asks.

"I don't think it could have been any longer," Mandy says, laughing.

"Come on, guys," says Leigh. "Tia has her own style. Her clothes are a little weird but she wears what she likes."

"Are you kidding?" says Mandy. "She looks like an old lady. She needs to get some style."

"Did you know that she designs and makes all of her own clothes?" asks Leigh.

"I didn't know that," says Ashley. "That's actually kind of cool."

"That is pretty cool," says Mandy. "I didn't know that about her. I wonder where she learned how to do that. Maybe she could teach me how to make something."

Photo courtesy of istockphoto.com © Chris Schmidt

1. Why are two of the girls making fun of Tia at the beginning of the story?

_____ a. They think her clothes are weird.

_____ b. They like long skirts.

_____ c. They are mad at Leigh.

2. How does Leigh feel about what Tia wears?

_____ a. She thinks Tia has her own style.

_____ b. She's proud of Tia's sewing skills.

_____ c. She's mad at her friends for making fun of Tia.

3. What made Ashley and Mandy change their opinions about Tia's clothes?

_____

_____

_____

Getting-Along Stories ❷

Read the story and answer the questions.

Suki and LeAnn are having a great time shopping together. They are looking for dresses for their graduation ceremony. Suki sees a dress in the window that she likes.

"Look at that, LeAnn, isn't it perfect? I can see me wearing that on graduation night."

"I don't know," LeAnn says. "It's kind of boring and ugly. You need something a little more colorful."

"What are you talking about?" asks Suki. "Maybe you're just jealous that I'll look really good in it."

"Hey, go ahead and buy it then," LeAnn says. "If you want to look boring, that's your choice."

1. Are these girls good friends? How can you tell? _____
   _____

2. LeAnn called the dress "boring and ugly." Which of these would have been a better way to state her opinion?

   _____ a. "That dress is okay, but I think you'd look better in something more colorful."

   _____ b. "Why do you always pick out the ugliest clothes? You really need my help."

3. Do you think these girls always argue? Why? _____
   _____

4. What do you think will happen next? _____
   _____

5. What could LeAnn have done at the end of the story to make sure the girls continue to get along? _____
   _____

Getting-Along Stories ❸

Read the story and answer the questions.

Tanner always has his guitar with him. He really likes to play and sing in front of other people.

Even though Tanner likes to play for an audience, he only knows a couple of songs and he doesn't play them very well. Everyone thinks Tanner is a good guy. His friends don't want to hurt his feelings, but they're getting tired of listening to his guitar playing all the time.

A friend says to you, "Tanner really likes you. Why don't you ask him to take it easy with the guitar playing? He'll listen to you. If he doesn't knock it off, someone is going to say something nasty to him and hurt his feelings."

1. Which statements are true?

    _____ a. Tanner is not very popular.

    _____ b. Tanner is not a good guitar player.

    _____ c. Most people like Tanner.

2. What would be the best thing to say to Tanner without hurting his feelings?

    _____ a. "Maybe you should learn to play a different instrument. The guitar gets kind of boring after a while."

    _____ b. "It's cool that you like to play the guitar, Tanner, but maybe you should just talk to your friends sometimes instead of playing all the time."

    _____ c. "Tanner, you're not a very good guitar player. You're probably a worse singer. People are tired of listening to you."

3. What might happen if you don't say anything to Tanner and he keeps playing in front of people?

    _____

    _____

    _____

Answer Key

Answers will vary on items and pages not listed.

Page 6
1. a. disappointed, disgusted, embarrassed
   b. He wanted to make a nice dinner but now he has nothing to serve.
2. a. proud, happy, relieved
   b. She might have played poorly or forgotten her music.
3. b, c
4. b
5. a, b

Page 8
1. a. disappointed, sad, angry
   b. He was looking forward to this date, and now it's ruined.
2. a. nervous, intense, anxious
   b. He really wants to make the shot and doesn't want to miss it.

Page 9
1. c
2. d
3. a
4. b

Page 11
1. a. –
   b. +
   c. +

2. a. +
   b. +
   c. –
3. a. +
   b. –
   c. +
4. a. –
   b. +
   c. +

Page 13
1. a. -
   b. +
2. a. +
   b. -
3. a. -
   b. +
4. a. +
   b. -
5. a. -
   b. +

Page 17
1. a. proud
   b. disappointed, embarrassed
   c. angry
2. a. overjoyed, thrilled
   b. tired, proud
   c. frustrated, angry, disappointed

Page 18
1. Kind
2. Unkind
3. Unkind
4. Kind
5. Kind
6. Unkind
7. Unkind
8. Kind
9. Kind
10. Unkind
11. Kind
12. Unkind
13. Unkind
14. Kind
15. Kind

Pages 19
1. b, d
2. a, b
3. b, c

Page 22
1. How long have your grandparents been married? Where is the party and what kind of food will you have? Who's coming to the party? How many people are coming?
2. Is there a problem? What's going on? Are we the only people who are doing this in the cafeteria? What would you like us to do?

Page 24
1. b, d
2. b, c

Page 25
1. a, c
2. a, d

Page 28
1. a. –
   b. +
   c. –
2. a. –
   b. –
   c. +
3. a. –
   b. +
   c. –
4. a. +
   b. –
   c. –

Page 29
1. a. –
   b. +
2. a. +
   b. –
3. a. –
   b. +

Page 31
1. a. +
   b. –
   c. +
2. a. –
   b. +
   c. +
3. a. +
   b. –
   c. +
4. a. –
   b. +
   c. +
5. a. +
   b. –
   c. +

Page 35
1. b, c
2. a, c
3. a, b
4. a, c

Page 37
1. a
2. a
3. They learned that Tia makes her own clothes.

Page 38
1. Yes, they're good friends because they're shopping together and having a good time.
2. a

Page 39
1. b, c
2. b